INSTEAD SAY THIS
FOR PARENTS DURING THE CORONAVIRUS PANDEMIC

By Kishon M. Whittier, PsyD, LP

Instead Say This...
For Parents during the Coronavirus Pandemic
Copyright © 2020 by Kishon M. Whittier
ISBN: 9780578673431

Dedicated to my husband for his support and for providing our family with security.

During a pandemic, we as parents may notice that we are at a loss for words when our children ask us questions. Or, we may find ourselves giving answers or saying things that may instill fear and confusion rather than comfort and clarity.

Because of the unprecedented nature of this time, it is understandable that we as parents are unsure of how to support our children, provide them with information appropriate to their developmental level, and establish feelings of security in our homes.

This book will provide options of what to say to our children during the current pandemic as well as during illness outbreaks in our communities and classrooms in a more normal time.

The format of this book is as follows: The page on the left is something we might say to our child. The page on the right offers an alternative that better supports our child's social-emotional development.

This pandemic is really scary.

Instead say…

How are you feeling about all the changes that the pandemic has caused?

OR, FOR YOUNGER CHILDREN

We are here to keep you safe.

Don't listen to what your friends are saying about the coronavirus.

Instead say…

I am glad you and your friends are able to talk about the coronavirus. If you ever wonder if what they are saying is accurate, let me know and we can talk about it.

OR, FOR YOUNGER CHILDREN

Your friend's parents talk to your them about the coronavirus and we will talk to you about it. Sometimes your friends may not remember things correctly.

We'll all probably get COVID-19 at some point.

Instead say...

Right now, it's important that as few people as possible get COVID-19 to allow medical facilities to not get overwhelmed with patients. They are working on a vaccine to prevent the disease in the future and they are working on medicines to ease the symptoms for those of us that may get it in the future.

OR, FOR YOUNGER CHILDREN

Right now, you don't have to worry about who will get COVID-19. We are doing everything possible to keep you safe.

People are making too big of a deal about this.

Instead say…

Because this is so different from anything we've been through in the past, it may feel like people are over-reacting; however, we need to listen to scientists, physicians, and other professionals in the field since they understand the situation the most.

OR, FOR YOUNGER CHILDREN

It is important to do what the doctors are telling us, like washing our hands and staying at home together.

People are not taking this seriously enough and it's going to get really bad!

Instead say...

I notice some people not following the mandates from the governor. What we can do is make sure we are doing what is recommended to keep ourselves and those around us safe.

OR, FOR YOUNGER CHILDREN

We need to do our part to keep ourselves and other people healthy.

You seem so anxious about the coronavirus. It's going to be fine.

Instead say…

I notice you seem more anxious lately. Would you say that is true? Would you be willing to talk with me about what's on your mind?

OR, FOR YOUNGER CHILDREN

You may be having more feelings with all these changes. I have been feeling more crabby lately, have you too?

How many times do I have to tell you? Wash your hands for 20 seconds and use soap!

Instead say…

We are all still working on getting in the habit of washing our hands more thoroughly. What could we do to help us remember the plan?

OR, FOR YOUNGER CHILDREN

Let's come up with a new plan together for washing our hands. What song would you like to sing while we wash? Twinkle, Twinkle Little Star or do you have another idea?

You do not want to get COVID-19. It's really bad.

Instead say…

The symptoms of COVID-19 can include a cough, fever, and trouble breathing.

OR, FOR YOUNGER CHILDREN

COVID-19 can make people have a cough, fever, and it can feel hard to breathe.

We're not going to be able to go anywhere for a long time.

Instead say…

The people in charge are saying that we should stay at our home unless we need to get food or go to the doctor. This will last several more weeks and they may add more time after that depending on how things are going.

OR, FOR YOUNGER CHILDREN

We know that right now people need to stay at home as much as possible. We don't know how long we will have to do this, but we will be able to go places again when they tell us it is okay.

I'm tired of being around you too!

Instead, say…

> We are used to having more time away from each other. Let's make sure we are all getting the space we need and some alone time too.

OR, FOR YOUNGER CHILDREN

> Mom/dad needs a break sometimes and it's important for you to take a break each day too, so your body and mind can rest.

You keep coughing...I bet you have the coronavirus.

Instead say…

                I notice you've been coughing more often. How are you feeling otherwise?

OR, FOR YOUNGER CHILDREN

                It's no fun to have a cough. Would you like a warm drink to soothe your throat?

Just give me some space! I can't play with you every second of the day!

Instead say…

I enjoy playing with you and I have things I need to do for my work and to take care of our home. Let's play a game after lunch. Deal?

Aren't you supposed to be doing something for e-school right now?

Instead say…

It may take a few days to get into the routine of e-school. What is your plan right now? Is there anything I can do to make it an easier transition?

You can't just watch tv all day!

Instead say...

Let's come up with a schedule to follow. There will be tv time in the schedule and there will be other activities to do too.

Trust me. This is not how I want to spend my days either!

Instead say...

I know this is a hard time and I know that we will get through this.

You've been so disrespectful/naughty lately! What is going on with you?

Instead say...

Sometimes when things change, it makes it harder to be respectful. Let's talk about all the things that have changed and how we can still be kind to each other.

I can't wait for you to go back to daycare/school!

Instead say...

I need a break for about 15 minutes in my room to calm down. I am really frustrated/angry right now.

Your mom/dad has it made. They get to work without interruption all day and I am stuck with you!

Instead say...

I am still getting used to how things are now. I might need a lot of breaks during the day. Can we agree that we each get a break whenever we need it?

No, you won't get sick.

Instead say…

We don't know who will get sick. The things we can do to make it much less likely that we will get sick is to wash our hands and stay at least 6 feet way from others until we know who might have the virus and who does not.

OR, FOR YOUNGER CHILDREN

We don't know who will get sick. We are going to help you stay healthy as best we can.

The illness caused by coronavirus is just like the flu.

Instead say…

While the illness has a few similarities to the flu, it is more dangerous for some people, like older people and people who are already sick with something else. And it seems to get passed on to other people more easily than the flu viruses. That's why we are being extra careful now.

OR, FOR YOUNGER CHILDREN

The coronavirus sickness is different from the flu and that is why we are doing different things to stay healthy.

Most people will die if they get the coronavirus/Nobody dies from the coronavirus.

Instead say…

Most people will be okay if they get the coronavirus illness (COVID-19). They will be very sick for a while, but most people do not die from it.

You probably will have to do school at home for a really long time.

Instead say…

We don't know how long you will do e-school. We are taking it week by week and month by month. We will keep learning more as time goes on, but it is not possible to know when things will return to a more typical routine.

No, I won't die if I get COVID-19.

Instead say...

If I get COVID-19, there is a really good chance that I will be just fine. I am not in the older age group and I don't have any other illnesses. But I am still going to be careful and follow all the rules to lessen my chances of getting sick.

OR, FOR YOUNGER CHILDREN

I am going to take care of myself to stay healthy.

Grandma won't die if she gets the coronavirus disease.

Instead say...

Since Grandma is older and she also has diabetes, she could get very sick and maybe even die if she gets COVID-19. But we are helping her stay safe by not visiting her in person right now and she is doing everything right to stay healthy.

OR, FOR YOUNGER CHILDREN

Grandma is going to take care of herself to stay healthy and we will help by not visiting her and keeping our germs away.

I don't know why that person is wearing a mask.

Instead say…

He is wearing a mask either because he is sick and doesn't want to get others sick or because he is trying to stay healthy. Some masks keep germs from spreading by blocking them from leaving the mask or blocking them from entering his mouth or nose.

OR, FOR YOUNGER CHILDREN

He is wearing a mask to protect himself from getting sick.

I know you miss your friends. I miss mine too.

Instead say…

This is a really hard time and I understand you miss your friends very much. What are some things you could do from home to feel closer to them?

OR, FOR YOUNGER CHILDREN

This is a really hard time and I understand you miss your friends. Maybe we could talk to them on the computer.

I think it's their fault that this coronavirus has become a pandemic.

Instead say...

It is no person or country's fault that this coronavirus has become a pandemic. Lots of things happened to lead to this and now each country in the world has to do their part to slow the spread of the disease.

I don't want to hear any more about the coronavirus or COVID-19 or the pandemic!

Instead say...

I am overwhelmed with talking about these things right now. I need to take a break from it until tomorrow. Can we agree to talk more about it then?

You need to talk about this with me. You can't pretend nothing is happening.

Instead say…

I am here if you ever have any questions or thoughts about everything that's going on. Is that okay if I check in with you once in a while to see how you are doing?

OR, FOR YOUNGER CHILDREN

I am going to take care of you. Let me know if you feel worried about anything or have any questions.

With everything that is happening, I am very worried about money. How are we going to pay our bills? Buy food?

Instead say…

Our jobs have changed and our financial situation will be less predictable for a while. That will mean we can't buy what we normally would. If we are thoughtful about it, we will be okay.

OR, FOR YOUNGER CHILDREN

Right now we have to be more careful about what we buy. We can't buy that toy today or anytime soon. Let's find a toy here at home that you haven't played with in a while.

Life as we know it is over.

Instead say…

Many things are very different now. Slowly things will settle down and life will feel more regular again.

www.ingramcontent.com/pod-product-compliance
Lightning Source LLC
Chambersburg PA
CBHW051150290426
44108CB00019B/2675